young
CHANGEMAKERS
CHAMPIONS
FOR CHANGE

Written By
STACY C. BAUER

Illustrated By
EMANUELA NTAMACK

This book is dedicated to DJ Annie Red, Lachlan, Addy, Izzy, Oliver, Bethany, Priscilla, Liam, Shirley, Annie, Maddy, Jayson, and Sammie. Thank you for sharing your inspirational stories with the world. You are true champions.

Champions for Change
Young Change Makers
Published by Hop Off the Press, LLC
www.stacycbauer.com

Minneapolis, MN

Book design by Travis D. Peterson.

Library of Congress Control Number: 2022901918
Bauer, Stacy C. Author
Ntamack, Emanuela Illustrator
Champions for Change

ISBN: 978-1-7373890-3-3

JUVENILE NONFICTION

Printed in China.

All inquiries of this book can be sent to the author.
For more information, please visit **www.stacycbauer.com**

MEET THE CHANGE MAKERS!

INSPIRATIONAL ICONS
Chasing their dreams and encouraging others to do the same!

HELPING HANDS
Delivering support to those in need.

ANIMAL AMBASSADORS
Helping and advocating for animals.

CONSERVATION CREW
Saving the planet.

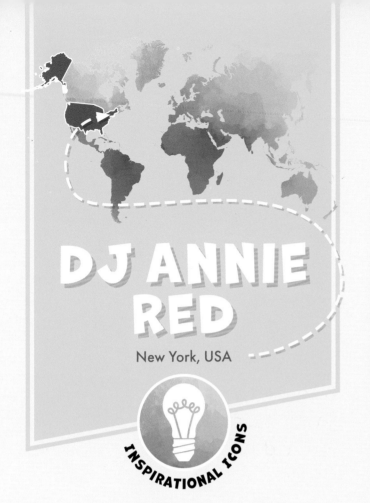

DJ ANNIE RED

New York, USA

"FIND OUT WHAT YOUR PASSION IS, SOMETHING YOU FEEL STRONGLY ABOUT, AND GO FOR IT!"

Have you ever been made fun of for being different? Samirah Ann Horton understands how you feel. When she was a young child, she stood out because she was different from most other girls. She liked blue instead of pink, had a deep voice, and was good at sports. Because of this, Samirah became a target for bullies. Instead of letting them hold her back, she decided to do something to help the fight against bullying.

Samirah always had a passion for music. Her dad, uncles, and grandparents had grown up in the **hip-hop** scene in New York. Her dad had even become a DJ! So it was only natural that Samirah would turn to music to create an anti-bullying message. When she was just six years old, she composed a rap song, "No You Won't Bully Me," and started calling herself DJ Annie Red (Ann is her middle name, and her nickname as a baby was Annie Red because her face was always red).

DJ Annie Red decided to pursue being a DJ like her father. She learned a lot about being a DJ from her dad and YouTube, but she also attended a special DJ school in Manhattan, New York—where she became the youngest graduate at just eight years old!

Since writing her first rap song, DJ Annie Red has written many more songs.

She travels around the United States, talking to students about bullying and performing her music for them. She also wrote a book about bullying. DJ Annie Red spreads her message all over social media and YouTube. Her original song has over 5,000 views. Kids who've been bullied have shared with her that she's made a difference in their lives. She has given kids who are bullied confidence and hope.

People sometimes don't take her seriously because of her age, but DJ Annie Red doesn't let that stop her. With the love and support of her parents, teachers, and friends, DJ Annie Red continues to have the confidence to use her voice and stand up against bullying.

HIP-HOP is a type of music. It is also a culture, or way of life. It includes many types of expression—for example, rapping, deejaying, dancing, and graffiti painting. Fans of hip-hop culture also wear certain styles of clothing.

young CHANGEMAKERS™
INSPIRATIONAL ICON!

- Stand up against bullying! If you see someone being made fun of, stop it! Tell a trusted adult or your friends.

- Be kind to others, no matter what.

- Visit DJ Annie Red on social media and buy her book to learn more about her mission. www.instagram. com/dj_annie_red

DJ ANNIE RED'S ADVICE FOR YOU:

Use your voice. Use all your platforms to live out your passion. If you have a passion, go for it!

DJ Annie Red with her father.

DJ ANNIE RED'S FUN FACTS:

- DJ Annie Red enjoys playing basketball and is a DJ for the Brooklyn Nets.

- She loves to build with Legos.

- She is a praise dancer at church.

LACHLAN

Ontario, Canada

HELPING HANDS

> "I DONATE TO THE HOSPITAL SO THE DOCTORS CAN HELP PEOPLE THAT ARE HURT."

Have you ever had a lemonade stand? When Lachlan Brown was just three years old, he decided it would be fun to have one. Lachlan's parents suggested he donate any money he raised to the local **hospital foundation** in order to help their community.

Lachlan is a natural-born entrepreneur–someone who decides to create or run a business. Entrepreneurs are often creative, daring people, and the businesses they operate provide jobs, goods, and services to communities. Lachlan loves talking to people and being a leader. All of these traits help him raise money. Since that first lemonade stand, Lachlan has built a great friendship with the hospital foundation director. He has participated in their **radiothon**, taken part in their parade float, been in videos, and asked for donations instead of birthday gifts. When other children see how someone so young is making such a difference, they are encouraged to do something too! Lachlan has invited friends to help with the lemonade stands and asked them to call in to the radiothon. There have been many children who have had roadside stands and donated the money they raised to the hospital because they heard about Lachlan doing it.

One of Lachlan's favorite things is when he's invited to the hospital and shown how the money he's donated is being used. His donations have helped buy hospital equipment, like a

Lachlan's Fun Facts:

- **Lachlan loves music. He plays piano.**

- **He enjoys dirt biking and fishing.**

- **He loves his younger brother Connor.**

new **ultrasound machine**, not provided by the government. Lachlan sees the connection between donating his hard-earned money and helping people in his community with their health.

Over the years, Lachlan has continued to work hard to raise money for the foundation. Last year, he was able to donate $450. He raised the money by making little campfire starters and selling them at local tourist campgrounds. Lachlan plans to keep donating in the future. He wants people to get the care that they need.

HOSPITAL FOUNDATION: A non-profit organization that supports the programs and services of a local hospital.

RADIOTHON: An event on the radio that helps raise money for a specific cause by taking pledges from people who call in.

An **ULTRASOUND MACHINE** has a microphone attached to a computer. It can listen to your insides and then sends these sounds to the computer which creates a picture!

BECOME A young CHANGEMAKERS™ HELPING HAND!

- **Have a lemonade stand to raise money for a cause you care about.**

- **Do odd jobs and donate the money you earn.**

- **Encourage others to find ways to do acts of kindness too!**

LACHLAN'S ADVICE FOR YOU:

Be a leader. It only takes a little step to make big change.

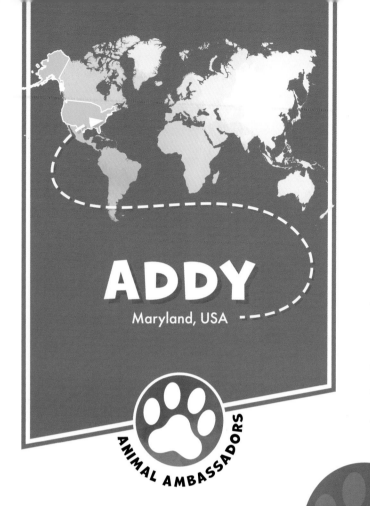

ADDY
Maryland, USA

ANIMAL AMBASSADORS

VEGETATION: plant life.

"GO LEARN, GO HELP, GO-RILLAS!"

Did you know that mountain gorillas are very similar to us? They laugh and show emotions just like we do! Addy Barrett was amazed when she found this out in a book she read in first grade. She also learned that mountain gorillas are endangered.

There are only 1,000 mountain gorillas left in the wild. Mountain gorillas are beautiful, majestic animals who live in Rwanda, Uganda, and the Republic of the Congo. The forest habitat they live in is shrinking as people cut down trees to create farmland. Mountain gorillas also lose their lives when they are caught in traps set for other animals and, because they are so closely related to humans, can catch our diseases.

Addy learned that mountain gorillas are very important to the forests they live in. When they trample through the forest, their bodies stomp down **vegetation**, allowing new growth to happen. They also help spread seeds through the forest. The more Addy researched and learned about the gorillas, the more

she grew to love and admire them. She decided to take action to try to help get them off the endangered species list.

When Addy was seven years old, she did bake sales and lemonade stands to raise money for the gorillas. She donated the money to the **Dian Fossey Gorilla Fund**. She wanted to do something more, so, with the help of her mom, Addy created a website and started designing t-shirts. Every time someone bought a shirt, Addy got pied in the face! She ended up getting pied over 100 times! This fundraiser caught the attention of one of the Fossey Fund board members, Dave Singer. Dave came out to meet Addy and thank her in person for helping the gorillas. He, and the entire Fossey Fund organization, have been a big support to Addy ever since. Addy also supports **The Ellen Fund** and has been named one of their three ambassadors.

Addy's next event to help the gorillas was her Gorilla Gala in 2018. She wanted to have a fun event that would raise money and encourage kids to get involved in helping gorillas. Guests were asked to donate five dollars to get in. The celebration included games, food, and a silent auction with items people could bid on that were donated by companies and businesses. They even had paintings for the auction that were done by actual gorillas! They have had three galas so far and raised over $15,000!

Addy plans to keep educating herself and others about the gorillas and other conservation projects in the future. She also aims to continue doing whatever she can to help. Even though she is young, she is making a difference, and she wants you to know that you can too!

The **DIAN FOSSEY GORILLA FUND** is a charity for the protection of endangered mountain gorillas. The fund (first named the Digit Fund after her beloved gorilla friend Digit) was created by Dr. Dian Fossey in 1978 for the sole purpose of financing her anti-poaching patrols and preventing further poaching of the mountain gorillas.

THE ELLEN FUND was founded in 2018 as a gift for Ellen DeGeneres, whose childhood hero was Dian Fossey. They support global conservation efforts for endangered species.

BECOME A

young CHANGEMAKERS™ ANIMAL AMBASSADOR!

- **Find an endangered animal you love, and research what you can do to help!**

- **Educate yourself about endangered species.**

- **Find out more about Addy and her organization Gorilla Heroes here:** facebook.com/gorillaheroes

ADDY'S ADVICE FOR YOU:
If you find something you're passionate about, let that be your focus! Focus on what you CAN do, not what you can't!

IZZY

Illinois, USA

INSPIRATIONAL ICONS

ONE SMALL ACT OF KINDNESS CAN CHANGE THE WORLD

LOVE IS HOPE AND BRINGS FREEDOM FROM DISEASE

"LOVE IS KINDNESS AND BRINGS FREEDOM FROM DISEASE."

Have you ever written a poem? When Izzy Sani was five, she learned about poet Maya Angelou. As she read Angelou's poetry, Izzy began thinking about how she could use her own words to make a sign to give hope and joy to people during the onset of the COVID-19 pandemic.

Izzy came up with a slogan: "Love is kindness and brings freedom from disease." Then she created a beautiful, colorful sign. Izzy wanted to try to sell the signs to raise money for charity. She and her mom talked about different places to donate the funds she raised. Izzy wanted to help kids her age, so they decided to donate the money

Izzy's Fun Facts:

- Izzy loves to go downhill skiing and can ride a chairlift by herself.

- She enjoys gymnastics.

- She likes reading.

- Izzy wants to be a lawyer to help make fair laws.

14

to the Ryan Banks Academy, a school that's helping kids from low-income families get a good education.

Her love for hearts, sunshine, and rainbows were the inspiration for the name of her project, Izzy's Rainbow World. Izzy's Rainbow World is intended to spread positive thoughts and teach others a life lesson while helping those in need.

Izzy's sign was the perfect way a five-year-old could make an impact. To help get the word out, Izzy made a video about her project, and her mom put the video on social media and contacted their friends and family all over the country. Izzy was even featured on the news! People started placing orders for yard signs, **car decals**, and cloth hanging signs. They found a printing shop to print people's orders and started sending them out.

With the help of her mom, Izzy has sold her signs to families across the country and raised awareness for the Ryan Banks Academy in a piece on the local news. So far, she has raised over $2,600 for the academy. She continues to have signs created. Izzy and her mom now use her signs on thank you cards in order to keep her project going.

BECOME A

young
CHANGEMAKERS™
INSPIRATIONAL ICON!

- **Make an encouraging card for someone.**

- **Write a kind message on someone's sidewalk or driveway with chalk.**

- **Make an inspiring sign and put it in your yard.**

CAR DECAL: A special sticker to put on a car.

IZZY'S ADVICE FOR YOU:

Make something, make copies, make a difference! Don't forget to be happy!

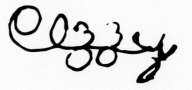

15

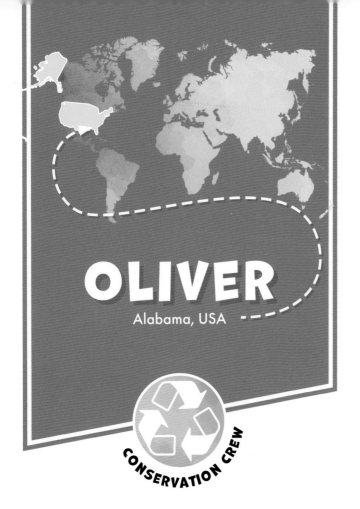

OLIVER

Alabama, USA

CONSERVATION CREW

"YOU CAN HELP
DO YOUR PART;
ON YOUR BEACH IS
WHERE YOU START."

Have you ever been to the ocean? Oliver Caver loves the beach. When he was just a toddler, during his family's daily walks on the beach, he noticed all of the garbage lying around. His parents began teaching him about the dangers of littering and **plastic pollution**.

Since oceans are lower than almost all land, a lot of our plastic ends up there, causing harm to sea life. Marine animals can get tangled in the trash or eat it by accident, poisoning themselves. Oliver loves sea creatures, especially ghost crabs and sea turtles, so when he saw bite marks in the trash that was washed up, he was very worried. Sea creatures were trying to eat the plastic! They also saw crabs on the beach pulling plastic toward their holes. It was then, at the age of four, that Oliver took action. He decided to do his part to protect the sea creatures by picking up trash. His mission was to clean up the beach and inspire others to do the same!

Oliver started bringing garbage bags on their beach trips and putting trash in them. His parents helped by establishing Clean Horizons to bring awareness to their mission and inspire others to clean up their beaches too. They also wrote a children's book about Oliver called *Litter, Litter, Please Come Here* to help teach children about plastic pollution and what they can do to help.

In that first year, Oliver and his family picked up over 4,000 pounds of trash! They organized beach cleanups and gave prizes to people who picked up the most litter. They have sponsored four community cleanup events so far and picked up over 16,000 pounds of trash in their area!

Oliver's favorite part about his journey so far is receiving letters from other kids saying they were inspired by him to clean up garbage in their area. Oliver plans on hosting more community cleanup events in the future, so he can work toward his goal of clean beaches all over the world!

What is plastic pollution? The buildup of plastic in our environment, which creates problems for wildlife and their habitats.

BECOME A young CHANGEMAKERS™ CONSERVATION CREW MEMBER!

- If you see litter, pick it up!

- Throw your garbage in the garbage can.

- Recycle when you can.

- When you're shopping, bring a reusable cloth bag instead of using plastic bags.

- Use a reusable water bottle instead of plastic water bottles.

- Check out Oliver's book and his website: cleanhorizons.org

OLIVER'S FUN FACTS:

- Oliver wants to be a farmer when he grows up.

- He loves to surf and play in the waves with his sister.

- Pizza and ice cream are his favorite foods.

- He is scared of snakes.

OLIVER'S ADVICE FOR YOU:

You can do anything with a little hard work. Find ways to make the work fun and it is really not like work at all!

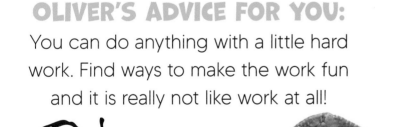

Horneyed Ghost Crab by John Dickens on Wikimedia Commons is licensed under CC BY 3.0.

BETHANY

Georgia, USA

HELPING HANDS

HAPPY BAGS

"CHILDREN HAVE
THE POWER TO
CHANGE THE WORLD."

19

Bethany's Fun Facts:

- Her favorite animal is a squirrel.

- She spends every moment she can outside in nature.

- Bethany enjoys camping, riding bikes, and playing games with her family.

- She loves to dance in the rain!

Meet Bethany Moultry, a little girl with a huge heart. When she was just five years old, Bethany was running errands with her mom when she saw some people standing on the streets holding signs asking for help. It broke her heart, and she immediately asked her mom what they could do.

They began by buying supplies they thought people would need. Then, they put them into quart-sized bags to give to homeless people in their area. They did this for six months, then her mom asked Bethany what she wanted for her sixth birthday. When Bethany said she wanted to help more people with her bags, they knew they needed to reach out for help. Bethany started writing letters to family and friends about her mission. Her mom created an Amazon Wish List and a Facebook page to help get the word out. Bethany named her project Bethany's Happy Bags because she wants the people receiving them to know she cares about them and hopes the bags make them happy.

Soon, they were getting so many donations, they moved up to gallon-sized bags! The bags included an encouraging card made by Bethany, a drink, hand sanitizer, food, body wipes, a first aid kit, and socks. They also added in other items depending on the season or how much room they had left.

There are more than 4,000 people experiencing homelessness in the city of Savannah, Georgia. Bethany and her mom are in contact with many agencies and shelters who help the homeless in their area. They post updated information about the homeless situation on their Facebook page. They want people everywhere to be aware of what's going on so they can help too.

Bethany and her mom pass out the happy bags in various ways. They drop some off with the police department and different homeless shelters in their city. They also keep some in their car in case they come across someone who needs one. They give them to their neighbors and friends who want to help distribute them. In the past year, Bethany has given out over 3,000 happy bags, and she plans to give out many more!

BECOME A

- **Find out how to help the homeless in your area.**

- **Put together some bags of food and other supplies and keep them in your car in case you come across someone who needs help.**

BETHANY'S ADVICE FOR YOU:

We all have the power within us to make a difference in the world, no matter what our age is. Ask a parent or trusted adult to help you raise money or purchase the supplies that you'll need to start!

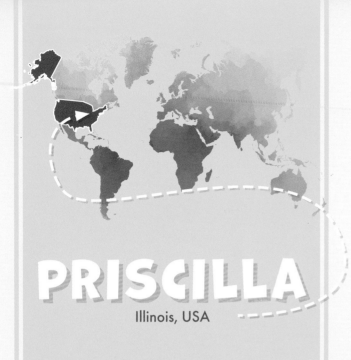

PRISCILLA

Illinois, USA

INSPIRATIONAL ICONS

"THE JOURNEY OF A LIFETIME STARTS WITH THE TURNING OF A PAGE."

Author Rachel Anders

Do you enjoy reading? Priscilla Leon has always loved to read. When she was nine, her love of reading inspired her to do something to make a difference in the world. She noticed that many kids were sharing and talking about their favorite toys online, but she really wanted to focus on books. She decided to share her love of books by reading to others on social media.

With the help of her mom, a **blogger**, Priscilla started an Instagram account where she read books aloud for other kids to enjoy. Her mom helped by asking authors to donate books for Priscilla to read. At first, she was shy and nervous about reading online. But, as she practiced and did it more and more, she became very comfortable reading.

Once Priscilla had a lot of people watching and listening to her read-alouds, she began raising money for charity. In return for hearing authors' books read on her account, she asked her viewers to donate to a charity. Priscilla loves animals and raised money for a local animal shelter. She also helped raise thousands of dollars for local children's hospitals.

Priscilla went out into her community to collect books to donate to Book First Chicago, an organization that creates libraries for **low-income schools**. It is important to her that every child has access to good books to read, especially if they don't have any books at home. Book First Chicago helps get books into kids' hands. Priscilla worked hard to collect thousands of books to donate to this organization.

Priscilla hopes to continue to collect more books for kids who need them, raise money for charity, and keep inspiring children to read! She even hopes to write her own children's book one day. Priscilla wants you to know that you should always follow your heart. You can find a way to help others through what you love to do!

A **BLOGGER** is someone who writes online.

LOW-INCOME SCHOOLS don't have as much money or opportunities as other schools.

BECOME A
young CHANGEMAKERS™
INSPIRATIONAL ICON!

- **Read a book to someone.**
- **Donate your old books or buy new books to donate.**
- **Find a charity you're passionate about and learn how you can help.**

PRISCILLA'S FUN FACTS:

- **Priscilla loves drawing.**
- **She enjoys riding horses.**
- **Her favorite food is chicken tenders.**
- **She dreams of becoming a veterinarian or a marine biologist.**

PRISCILLA'S ADVICE FOR YOU:

Always follow your heart and do what you love.

LIAM

Massachusetts, USA

HELPING HANDS

"EVERYONE DESERVES A LITTLE
KINDNESS IN THEIR LIVES."

Have you ever felt bored during your long summer break? When Liam Hannon was ten years old, and looking for something to do that summer, he and his dad found Brain Chase, an online program that provides weekly challenges for kids. Liam's first challenge was to help people experiencing homelessness.

Liam's father suggested they rent a food truck and drive all over the city to feed the homeless, but Liam noticed there were people who needed help right outside his own apartment. The next week, Liam made twenty lunches (peanut butter and jelly sandwiches, granola bars, and water) and handed them out to people who were hungry.

And Liam didn't stop there! He launched a program called Liam's Lunches of Love—which is a kindness project as well as a food one! What started as a summer project is now a year-round endeavor. Liam's lunches are packed in brown paper bags, which are decorated with kind and encouraging words and pictures. The first time Liam handed

LIAM'S FUN FACTS:

- **Liam loves musical theater and acting.**

- **He enjoys designing phone wallpapers of his favorite fictional characters.**

- **He loves spreading kindness!**

out lunches, he and his mom decorated the bags. Now, Liam gets brown paper bags sent to him from all over the country! One school in Oregon recently sent him 500 decorated bags! Liam's ultimate goal is to spread *kindness* to people through his lunches.

Liam with his solar-powered wagon.

Liam delivers the lunches in a couple of different ways. He has a small wagon to pile bins on. Liam, and the friends and family who are helping him, pull the wagon on a specific route to find people who need food. They also have a bigger solar-powered wagon for when they serve hot food. This wagon can hold 2,000 pounds and keeps the food warm. Liam and his volunteers set tables out in front of his apartment building to serve people in the community.

In the five years since Liam's Lunches of Love began, he's served over 15,000 lunches to people in his community experiencing homelessness. Liam plans on continuing this project in the future or possibly passing the project on to another child who might be interested in making a difference too!

BECOME A

young CHANGEMAKERS™ HELPING HAND!

- **Visit Liam's website and see how you can help:** www.liamslove.com

- **Write notes or letters of encouragement for people who are struggling.**

- **Donate food to your local food shelf.**

LIAM'S ADVICE FOR YOU:
Start small, do something that you care about, and get your friends and family involved.

Liam

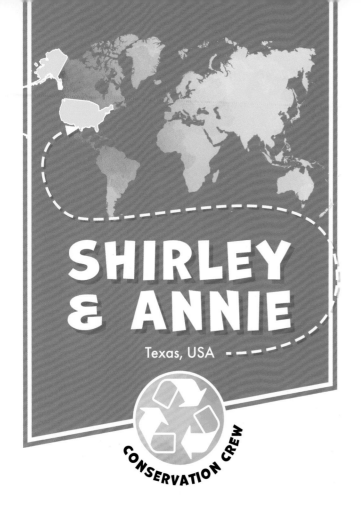

SHIRLEY & ANNIE

Texas, USA

CONSERVATION CREW

"THE HOUSTON RESIDENTS WHO LIVE IN FOOD DESERTS DON'T MERELY MAKE UP A STATISTIC; THEY ARE PEOPLE WHO DESERVE TO HAVE ACCESS TO BASIC NEEDS."

Did you know that food takes up more space in United States landfills than anything else? Americans throw away more food than any other country in the world, about 30-40% of our entire food supply—almost 80 billion pounds each year! That adds up to be about 219 pounds per person. That's like each person throwing more than 650 apples into the landfill!

Food waste hurts the environment and wastes money. Think about all of the water it takes to grow and produce food—and one-third of it gets thrown away! Rotting food in landfills also creates poisonous gasses that harm our planet and contribute to **climate change**.

Sisters Annie and Shirley Zhu didn't know all of this either when they volunteered to help a grocery store recover after a hurricane damaged it in Houston, Texas. They were shocked when they learned how much good food is thrown away, especially since there are so many people who need it. They discovered that 25% of the people living in Houston live in food deserts, which means they have limited access to a variety of healthy foods.

That, along with the fact that so much food is wasted, inspired them to take action. They decided to try to get the wasted food to the people who need it.

Shirley and Annie got a group of students together at their school who wanted to help. After five months of planning and preparation, their nonprofit, **Fresh Hub**, held its first monthly market event. Second Servings, a food rescue service in Houston, connected them with several local bakeries and grocery stores. Fresh Hub volunteers rescued unsold food from those stores and bakeries before it was thrown away and gave it to people who needed it.

Fresh Hub has carried out over 21 food rescue markets since 2018. They have rescued 14,700 pounds of food from stores and served over 1,830 people living in Houston. Annie and Shirley also created the Fresh Hub app with two other students. This app helps people living in food deserts lead healthy lifestyles by connecting them to Fresh Hub markets and teaching them about healthy eating.

Climate Change describes a change in the typical weather of a region–such as high and low temperatures and the amount of rainfall–over a long period of time.

The girls say the best part of what they do is meeting the people they've helped and seeing their faces light up when they get fresh food for their families. Every family deserves to go to sleep full of good, healthy food. When they go away to college, Shirley and Annie plan to keep their charity going by passing it on to younger high school students.

young CHANGEMAKERS™ CONSERVATION CREW MEMBER!

- Learn how to compost your food scraps to keep them out of landfills.

- Read the expiration labels on your food to keep from throwing away food that's still good. Dates with the word "best" (best by) just means the food may not taste the best, but the food is still fine to eat.

- Freeze food that you can't eat right away so you can eat it later.

- Plan your meals and make a grocery list so you don't overbuy.

SHIRLEY AND ANNIE'S ADVICE FOR YOU:

Set small goals and do it step by step.

SHIRLEY AND ANNIE'S FUN FACTS:

- Shirley's favorite food is mangoes.

- Her hobbies include painting, singing karaoke, and knitting.

- She enjoyed her trip to Spain and China.

- Annie's favorite food is apples.

- Her hobbies include dancing and painting.

- She loved traveling to Japan and China.

MADDY

Minnesota, USA

INSPIRATIONAL ICONS

SIGNING UP TO SAVE LIVES

"I DON'T WANT ANY OTHER CHILD TO GO THROUGH WHAT I WENT THROUGH."

When Maddy Tax was 15 years old, she was diagnosed with Hodgkin's Lymphoma, a cancer found in the **lymph nodes** on both sides of her neck and in her lungs. A month later, she started treatment. After each treatment, she was tired, feverish, and weak. She no longer had the energy to hang out with friends, and the medicine caused her hair to fall out in clumps until she had nothing left.

Maddy went through four months of treatments and was finally pronounced cancer-free!

A few weeks later, the Leukemia and Lymphoma Society, a charity supporting people who have certain cancers, asked Maddy to run as a candidate for their Student of the Year fundraising campaign. At first, she wasn't sure about doing it. After going through those challenging months of treatment, Maddy just wanted to be done thinking about and talking about her sickness, but, in the end, she decided that she wanted to raise awareness and support others. She wanted to do something to help kids who were fighting a battle similar to hers. It was the right decision. Not only did her fundraising experience end up helping others, it helped her come to terms with her experience.

The seven-week fundraiser raised money for blood cancer research for better treatments, education, and, hopefully, cures. While running the fundraiser, Maddy educated others about blood cancers. Her community rallied behind her and

LYMPH NODES are small bean-shaped structures that are part of the body's immune system. They store white blood cells which help fight infection and disease.

helped spread the word about her campaign. She did some local events for the fundraiser and watched her community grow even closer. She discovered how many other people's lives are affected by cancer, especially young children. The fundraiser helped Maddy realize that she wasn't alone.

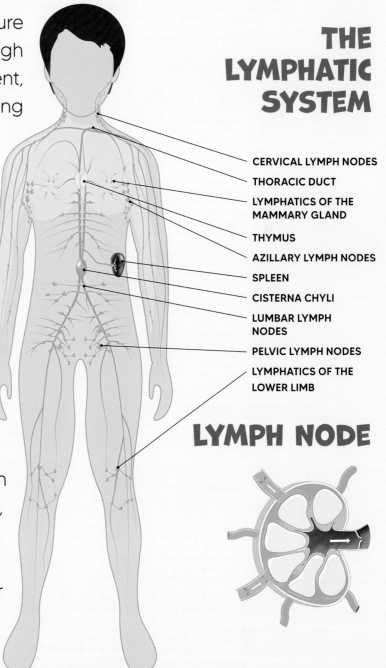

THE LYMPHATIC SYSTEM

CERVICAL LYMPH NODES
THORACIC DUCT
LYMPHATICS OF THE MAMMARY GLAND
THYMUS
AZILLARY LYMPH NODES
SPLEEN
CISTERNA CHYLI
LUMBAR LYMPH NODES
PELVIC LYMPH NODES
LYMPHATICS OF THE LOWER LIMB

LYMPH NODE

Some of the things Maddy and her team did to raise money included: selling cinnamon rolls, hosting a basketball tournament, and holding competitions at local elementary schools. Maddy remembers how one little boy told her proudly how he raised $60 for the fundraiser by walking dogs!

Maddy and her team ended up raising over $65,000. She was humbled by all of the people who came together to help during her fundraiser and inspired by the fact that anyone can make a difference.

MADDY'S FUN FACTS:

- **Pigs are her favorite animal, so much so that she doesn't eat pork.**

- **She loves the color green.**

- **She plans to major in musical theater in college!**

- **Maddy is left-handed.**

BECOME A young CHANGEMAKERS™ INSPIRATIONAL ICON!

- **Save up some of your money and donate it to a good cause.**

- **Research different walks in your area and participate!**

MADDY'S ADVICE FOR YOU:

Always remember that one small person can do huge things! If you want to help, don't be scared of the challenges that may come with helping. Face them head on.

Madelyn

JAYSON

TEXAS, USA

ANIMAL AMBASSADORS

"YOU'RE NEVER TOO YOUNG TO MAKE A DIFFERENCE."

Do you love animals? Do you have any pets? Jayson Kimberly has had eleven pets throughout his life (eight dogs and three cats) and has always been passionate about animals.

When Jayson was eleven years old, he decided to collect new and gently used items such as blankets, treats, toys, and leashes to take to animal rescues and shelters. He named his project Leave It for the Pooch because he thought he would be collecting mostly dog items. After he created a Facebook page, people started donating items. He was excited by his very first donation: 75 brand-new leashes and harnesses!

During the next few years, Jayson started several smaller service projects within Leave it for the Pooch. He called one of those Pennies Four Paws. When people donate money to Pennies Four Paws, the funds are used to help injured stray animals get the veterinary care they need.

When an animal rescue donated a shirt of theirs for Jayson to wear, he came up with another idea: he would wear shirts from animal shelters to school to teach his peers about the **overpopulation of homeless animals**! Soon, Jayson was getting shirts from states all over the United States and even other countries! He then had a quilt made with the shirts, which was auctioned off to raise funds for the shelters who participated.

Jayson had a live event called Draws for Paws in which he chose which rescue or shelter received funds from the quilt auction. Pavel Abromov, a Russian child artist who paints people's pets in exchange for supplies for his animal shelters, sent a few art pieces for the auctions too. Jayson raised $20,000 for local shelters and rescues in his last two auctions!

Jayson's newest project is called Save & Shine. Jayson collects realistic stuffed animals and takes them to elementary school classes where he talks about fostering and adoption. Each child gets a "foster pet" for the day (the stuffed animal). They name their pet and write about how to care for them and what their pet likes to do. Pictures are taken of the child with their foster pet, and then the profiles and animals are collected to go to phase two: the adoption event at local nursing homes. At the event, the

OVERPOPULATION OF HOMELESS ANIMALS: On any given day in the United States, there are an estimated 70 million homeless dogs and cats. This is happening mainly because of people abandoning their animals or allowing their animals to have babies over and over again. Many animals end up on the streets because shelters don't have enough room for them. They freeze, starve, get hit by cars, and get sick with preventable diseases.

nursing home residents receive a "pet" from one of the youth fosters. Jayson takes pictures of the resident adopters with their new pets, and then returns the folders to the school for students to open to see if their foster pet was adopted or will be attending another event. The reality is not all pets get adopted at their first adoption event. He loves seeing the joy of the children and elderly people as they learn about fostering and adoption in this fun and unique way.

BECOME A young CHANGEMAKERS™ ANIMAL AMBASSADOR!

- **Adopt a pet from an animal shelter instead of buying one.**

- **Spay or neuter your pets.**

- **Visit Jayson's website and donate to his cause:** leaveitforthepooch.com

- **Learn more about fostering animals.**

Jayson

JAYSON'S FUN FACTS:

- **His favorite food is Alfredo pasta.**

- **His favorite hobby is drumming.**

- **He has a fear of heights.**

- **Jayson's favorite animal is a dog.**

- **Jayson currently has three cats (Edison, Lily, and Little Bear), four fish, and two dogs (Heartley and Sampson).**

JAYSON'S ADVICE FOR YOU:

1. Find something that you enjoy and think about how you can make a difference.

2. Start small. Don't try some extravagant event because you will get overwhelmed and not want to continue. Try focusing on something small and start there.

3. Get friends and family who you enjoy being around involved too, they can help you become even more motivated.

BUDDY BENCH

CAPS for a CAUSE

> **"YOU DON'T JUST HAVE TO BE AN ADULT TO MAKE A DIFFERENCE. YOU CAN BE A KID TOO."**

Do you ever notice kids who don't have anyone to play with at recess? When Sammie Vance was eight years old, she heard about "buddy benches" at church camp. Buddy benches are places where kids can sit if they don't have anyone to play with at recess or on the playground. When other kids see someone on the buddy bench, they can invite that person to play with

them! Since Sammie had noticed lonely kids at her school before, she thought getting buddy benches for her school would be a great idea.

Sammie drew a picture illustrating what a buddy bench was all about and met with the principal to share her idea. He was excited to support her. Her mom found a company that makes benches out of plastic caps and lids called Green

Tree Plastics. Sammie thought this was a great idea because it would help the environment too!

Sammie needed to save 400 pounds of caps for every six-foot bench for her school's playground. That's about 19,000 caps!

Knowing she couldn't do it alone, Sammie organized a community-wide event to collect the caps. She shared her idea on social media and created a page where people could follow her progress. She spoke to the PTA (Parent-Teacher Association) at her school and got the rest of the school on board. Local businesses saved their caps for her. She and her friends even collected the caps of water bottles from the runners in a local marathon! Her community came together to help bring Sammie's dream to life.

Sammie then had a great idea for another goal–to collect a lid from each state! As word spread about this goal, she not only got some from every state in the United States, she also received caps from Mexico, Afghanistan, Germany, and Africa!

After Sammie was featured on television and in newspapers, her story spread even further. People started sharing stories of how they were bullied as children and how much they loved Sammie's idea. Even *more* strangers started collecting and donating caps!

After only two months, Sammie had collected and sorted almost 80,000 caps, enough to get four buddy benches for her school!

Since then, she has helped over 150 groups all around the United States get buddy benches. She has also spoken to groups all over the country about the importance of kindness and recycling. Because she collects plastic caps and uses them to make the benches, Sammie has saved thousands of pounds of plastic from going into oceans or landfills. She has also helped her city's parks department collect 2,200 pounds of plastic caps for eleven buddy benches to go into parks all over the city!

Sammie's story proves that it only takes one small step from one person to make a difference! Since then, Sammie has brought kindness to thousands of kids all over the world through her book *Inspire the World: A Kid's Journey to Making a Difference* and her podcast Sammie Smiles, which features other young people making a difference.

SAMMIE'S FUN FACTS:

- Sammie loves wearing glasses.

- She is really good at hula-hooping.

- She thinks New York-style cheese pizza is the best!

- Her favorite color is teal.

When you see someone sitting on the buddy bench...

1. Start by saying hello. If you don't know the person, introduce yourself.

2. Make conversation. "What's up?" "How are you?"

3. Ask them to play with you or suggest an activity you can do together.

4. Don't make it the last time you hang out. Keep playing with your new friend.

BECOME A young CHANGEMAKERS™ HELPING HAND!

- If you see someone alone at recess, ask them if they want to play.

- If you don't have a buddy bench at your school, talk to your principal about getting one.

- Visit Sammie's website or purchase her book to learn more about her mission: sammiesbuddybenchproject.com

SAMMIE'S ADVICE FOR YOU:

You can start small. One kind act can make a big difference. One small thing can make a big difference. Mine started with one small bottle cap.

♡, Sammie

STACY C. BAUER

A native of Minneapolis, MN, Stacy C. Bauer is a wife, teacher, mother of two and owner of Hop Off the Press—a publisher of quality children's books. Along with self publishing her own books, Stacy enjoys helping aspiring authors realize their dreams. She is hoping to inspire people around the world to make a difference with her newest endeavor, nonfiction book series *Young Change Makers*. For more information and to check out Stacy's other books including her children's picture books, visit www.stacycbauer.com.

EMANUELA NTAMACK

Emanuela Ntamack is an artist and children's book illustrator, a beloved wife and mother. She is married to her Cameroonian husband Alix, and together they have two boys. She has been drawing continuously ever since she could hold a pencil. Growing up, she studied Art and Design in school and university. After she became a mother, she discovered her love for children's books illustrations. One of the biggest satisfactions of her work is when children—including her own—are inspired by the illustrations that she creates. She is thankful to God for the gift of art, and for the diversity and the beauty of Creation, which is a never-ending source of inspiration.